Character Encyclopedia

Written by
Catherine Saunders

Contents

Welcome to the Juice Bar, Andrea!

Characters

Heartlake City is a great place to visit, but it's an even better place to live. These happy residents love it here. Come and meet them and learn about their personalities, pastimes, and friendships.

Olivia

Olivia is a science genius—she loves inventing, building, and discovering how things work. Her friends are in awe of her amazing brain, but she's sweet and fun, too. When she's not in her workshop, Olivia likes to explore nature.

Top secret!

Olivia's best subjects at school are science and math, but she wishes she could be better at writing stories, like Stephanie.

Chemical beaker

Casual outfit

New discoveries

Olivia loves being outdoors, especially when science or maps are involved. She likes to discover new facts, such as the names of interesting trees.

Mia

Mia is an animal lover and is happiest when she's riding her horse, Bella. She likes to be outdoors—whether it's kayaking, skateboarding, or mountain biking. Mia is also caring and kind, and will look after anyone or anything that needs her help.

All about me

Hair color: Red

Eye color: Hazel

Favorite color: Green

Favorite food: Beet chips, ice cream

Hobbies: Horseback riding, magic, skateboarding, playing drums

Favorite animals: Bella (my horse), Charlie (my puppy), Felix (my cat)

Grooming brush

I love taking care of animals.

Charlie

Animal lover

Animals are very important to Mia and she often helps out at the Heartlake Vet Center and the stables. She dreams of becoming a vet or an animal psychologist.

7

Emma

Emma is buzzing with creativity, from fashion and interior design, to knitting and jewelry-making. She is not afraid to make bold fashion choices and loves to help others feel good about themselves, even her pets!

All about me

Hair color: Black

Eye color: Dark green

Favorite color: Purple

Favorite food: Chocolate

Hobbies: Design, craft, horseback riding, karate

Favorite animals: Lady (my poodle), Jewel (my cat), Robin (my horse)

> I designed this outfit myself!

Ideas center

Emma works hard in her design studio. First she sketches her ideas, then she photographs them. Finally, she cuts and sews pieces of fabric to bring her designs to life.

Top secret!

Emma's newest hobby is photography. She finds nature inspiring—whether it's a close-up of a leaf, a detailed sand pattern, or a silky spider's web.

Purse coordinates with outfit

8

Stephanie

All about me

Hair color: Blonde

Eye color: Blue

Favorite color: Pink

Favorite food: Anything homemade

Hobbies: Writing, soccer, learning to play electric guitar

Favorite animals: Daisy (my rabbit) and Coco (my neighbor's dog)

Playing soccer, flying a seaplane, or baking cupcakes—whatever Stephanie does, she likes to be in charge. She might seem a little bossy, but Stephanie is a loyal and supportive friend.

Cute summer outfit

Chocolate, strawberry, and vanilla slice

Birthday party

Super-organized, smart, and a natural leader, Stephanie is the go-to girl for party planning. She never forgets her friends' birthdays and spoils them with surprises and homemade cakes.

Did you know?
Stephanie edits the school magazine, *The Heartlaker*. She's getting all her friends involved, too.

Pink shoes

Andrea

Andrea is a born performer and dreams of becoming a singing superstar. She knows it will take hard work, as well as talent, so Andrea practices every day and saves the wages from her part-time job at the City Park Café to buy sparkly stage outfits.

Pitch perfect

Andrea is a talented dancer and actor, but singing is her passion. She writes all her own songs and loves to perform them—on stage, at school, or just into a ketchup bottle at the City Park Café.

Even Andrea's clothes have musical notes on them!

Did you know? Andrea writes a blog, *Andrea's Alley*, in which she shares her thoughts with online friends around the world.

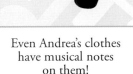

Light-pink flip-flops

10

Kate

Energetic Kate is always on the move. She loves planning adventures: From climbing the highest peaks in the Clearspring Mountains, to spending a night in the creepiest part of the Whispering Woods, Kate is ready for anything.

Wavy black hair

I'm all set for a beach adventure!

Stylish jet-ski outfit

Top secret!

Some of Kate's schemes can be a little crazy, like the time she climbed onto the roof of a fancy restaurant in Heartlake City.

Beach fun

Kate's favorite place is Ambersands Beach. She loves jet-skiing, surfing, and snorkeling, often with her friend, Stephanie.

Flippers for snorkeling

Andrew

Andrew is a straight-A student, he is good at sports, and he works for the Heartlake High TV station in his spare time. However, sometimes he can be a bit too eager to be the best at everything and he forgets how to be a good friend.

On the water

Andrew loves the ocean and joins Mia and Maya on a dolphin research mission on the *Dolphin Cruiser* boat. Andrew and Maya take time off to water-ski.

Let's hit the water everyone!

Polo shirt with nautical motif

Did you know? Andrew has known Emma, Andrea, and Stephanie since elementary school—they played soccer together.

Sensible deck shoes

Ella

Fun-loving Ella might be the queen of practical jokes at Heartlake Stables, but she takes horseback riding seriously. She never misses Summer Riding Camp and always listens to what Theresa teaches her.

Favorite horse
Ella has a special bond with energetic Champion, who jokes around, like Ella. Ella not only loves riding her, but also enjoys grooming her and feeding her carrots.

I'm always horsing around!

Pink halter top

All about me

Hair color: Black

Eye color: Dark green

Favorite color: Lilac

Favorite food: Veggie burger

Hobbies: Making ceramics, computer animation, horseback riding

Favorite animal: Champion, the horse

White cropped pants

Top secret!
Once Ella and her best friend Katharina switched the salt and sugar in the school cafeteria. Poor Olivia put salt in her tea!

Pale-pink flip-flops

13

Liza

Liza's passion is gardening and she is a keen member of her school's Farm Club. She loves to spend time with her cousin Mia at Sunshine Ranch, helping with farm work. Adventurous Liza also likes exploring the farm, to find special hangouts.

Close cousins

Liza is a year younger than Mia, and she looks up to her cousin. Mia is so caring and has such great friends, Liza wants to be just like her.

All about me

Hair color: Blonde

Eye color: Blue

Favorite color: Navy blue

Favorite food: Roasted vegetables, fresh fruit salad

Hobbies: Gardening, exploring

Favorite animal: Cotton, the lamb

Homegrown carrot

Black riding boots

Did you know?

Liza is very practical. She's good at building and fixing things.

Maya

Ever since the first time she went sailing, Maya has been boat crazy. She loves exploring the wide blue ocean, so when she won a contest to join the *Dolphin Cruiser* dolphin research mission, it was a dream come true.

Mission mates

On the Dolphin Research Mission, Maya made a new friend, Mia. Maya is an expert sailor and Mia is an animal expert, so together they make a great team.

> All hands on deck!

All about me

Hair color: Black

Eye color: Brown

Favorite color: Ocean blue

Favorite food: Grilled cheese sandwiches and green salad

Hobbies: Sailing, waterskiing, playing the trumpet

Favorite animals: Milo and Sheen, the dolphins

Tankini with matching sarong

Top secret!

Maya has heard that Mia is setting up a band—she'd like to join. Maya is a wonderful trumpeter and loves to be the center of attention.

Magenta-and-navy-blue flip-flops

Christina

Christina and Olivia have been friends since they were babies. The girls don't see each other very often any more, but their families often spend the winter holidays together in a cozy lodge at Clearspring Mountain.

Special delivery

Every year, Christina and Olivia take to the snow in a sled and deliver presents and cards to their neighbors—it's their special tradition!

Wavy blonde hair

Holiday-themed outfit

All about me

Hair color: Light blonde

Eye color: Dark green

Favorite color: Red

Favorite food: Chocolate cake

Hobbies: Playing the piano, swimming

Favorite animal: Sally (my hamster)

Did you know?
Christina loves dressing up. She always throws a costume party for her birthday. Olivia dresses as Einstein every year.

Black snow boots

Chloe

Mia's childhood friend, Chloe, is president of the Heartlake High Archaeology Club. She has a passion for history and loves to explore the ancient ruins around Heartlake City, looking for interesting artifacts.

Antique crown

Top secret!
Chloe loves to read books about Dark-Eyed Kate, a legendary pirate who once sailed the seas near Heartlake Harbor.

White tank top with pink and silver details

All about me

Hair color: Dark brown

Eye color: Green

Favorite color: Silver

Favorite food: Pot roast, toasted marshmallows

Hobbies: Archaeology, reading, ballroom dancing

Favorite animal: Spurrtacus (my cat)

Precious jewel found hidden in cave

Field trip

When Chloe found a dusty treasure map in her grandmother's attic, she set off on a thrilling adventure with Mia. They built a raft and found a cave with some dazzling jewels inside!

Nicole

Nicole is an old friend of Olivia's from before she moved to Heartlake City. Although it can be hard to keep in touch, they have remained close friends. Nicole keeps Olivia up-to-date with her adventures via text, email, and video chat.

Summer trip

Nicole is an outdoor girl and loves to go camping with Olivia. They go surfing, cycling, and searching for animal prints. They end the day singing around the campfire.

Top secret!

Olivia has told Nicole all about her new friends. Nicole secretly thinks that she would like outdoorsy Mia the best!

Summery halter top

Picnic basket

All about me

Hair color: Black

Eye color: Dark green

Favorite color: Yellow

Favorite food: Blueberry pancakes

Hobbies: Surfing, mountain biking, jogging

Favorite animal: Mikey (my cat)

Matthew

Matthew is one of the most popular students at Heartlake High. He is on the basketball team and writes a comic strip for the school magazine. After school, Matthew likes to head to the beach or hang out at the skate park.

> I've got some great new skateboard tricks.

Lime-green polo shirt

Dark-blue pants

Did you know?
Matthew and Mia have bonded over their shared interest in skateboarding.

Guitar guy

Matthew loves music, too. He's been learning the guitar for years and he would love to start a rock band.

Danielle

Danielle's family own the Downtown Bakery and she has helped out there ever since she was old enough to hold a mixing spoon. These days Danielle prefers playing volleyball to baking bread, but she hasn't told her parents.

Stop by the bakery for some tasty treats.

Lilac and navy outfit

Helping a friend

Danielle thinks that Mia is really cool. When she heard that her friend needed a part-time job, she got her one at the Bakery. Unfortunately, Mia isn't a natural baker.

Top secret!

Danielle would love to go horseback riding with Mia, but she has been too shy to ask. She will work up the courage one day!

Purple shoes

Katharina

It's never hard to find Katharina—she spends most of her time at Heartlake Stables. When she's not riding her horse, Niki, she helps Freya, the owner, train the other horses, or hangs out with her horse-mad friend, Ella.

Black riding helmet

Stylish riding jacket

Top team

Katharina spends hours every day practicing with Niki. Their specialties are jumping and dressage—elegant moves and fancy footwork that require a close partnership between the rider and horse.

Did you know?
Ella thinks Katharina needs to take time out from the stables, so she's teaching her friend how to make ceramics.

Black riding boots

Lily

Sporty Lily is determined to be the best at everything. She's the queen of the ice and every year she stars in the Heartlake Holiday Ice Spectacle. When she's not at the rink, Lily captains the Heartlake High volleyball team.

Ice-skating is my passion.

Warm sweater

Top secret!

Lily is popular, but she sometimes wishes she had more close friends. She finds it hard not to see her friends as competition.

Hot chocolate time

Lily is so focused on her goal that her friends often have to encourage her to relax. Stephanie meets her at the holiday market for delicious hot chocolate.

Ice skates

Isabella

Isabella is a huge music fan — she's a talented singer and is learning to play guitar. She has lots in common with her friend, Andrea. They met on their first day at elementary school and have been friends ever since.

> Let's give a concert at the pool!

Flower garland, also known as lei

Magenta sarong

Pool pals

Isabella and Andrea also share a love of hanging out at the Heartlake City Pool. Isabella is a strong swimmer and wants to become a lifeguard.

Did you know? Isabella and Andrea often sing *a cappella*, which means without any instruments accompanying them.

Julian

Julian has lots of interests: He loves singing, acting, drawing, and swimming. However, he often feels awkward in social situations and sometimes says the wrong thing. Julian's friends don't get offended though—they know that he has a kind heart!

Hooded zip-up sweater

At the mall

Julian has a part-time job in the computer and toy store at the Heartlake Shopping Mall. After work he often hangs out with his friends. Today, Emma and Stephanie are helping him pick out a new skateboard.

Did you know?
Julian is an adventurous person and likes to explore downtown Heartlake City in his free time.

Julian's new skateboard

24

Hair color: Blonde

Eye color: Blue

Favorite color: Red

Favorite food: Mexican food, especially tacos

Hobbies: Playing the cello, sledding, chess

Favorite animal: Charlie (Mia's puppy)

Ewa

Music-loving Ewa has been playing the cello for five years. She practices every day and often performs with the Heartlake Youth Orchestra (HYO). Despite her busy schedule, Ewa loves to take time off in the holidays to have fun with her friends.

Fantastic! It's starting to snow!

Stylish but warm sledding outfit

New band member?

Ewa is friends with Stephanie and Mia. Stephanie used to play violin for the HYO, where she met Ewa. Mia thinks Ewa would be great in the band she is setting up.

Top secret!

Ewa has a secret passion for computer games. She loves role-playing games and plays online with friends from all over the world.

Fake-fur-lined boots

25

Naya

When she's not whipping up tasty fresh drinks at the Heartlake Juice Bar, Naya can be found surfing the waves at Ambersands Beach. She's a free spirit and the girls admire her fun attitude.

Juice maestro

Naya takes pride in her work—she spends ages concocting the perfect juice and making it look fabulous.

Cell phone

All about me

Hair color: Blonde

Eye color: Hazel

Favorite color: Green

Favorite food: My special kale, lemon, and ginger juice

Hobbies: Surfing, playing the saxophone

Favorite animal: Bubbles, the turtle

Top secret!

Naya is considering her career options. She thinks she might like to travel the world, helping people in need.

Basket

Magenta ballet-style pumps

Robert

Heartlake High student Robert is a quiet, thoughtful person. He likes sketching, making his own movies, and listening to new music. However, Robert's favorite hobby is horseback riding with his best friend Major, the horse.

Blue riding helmet

Winner's trophy

Did you know?
Robert has a part-time job teaching young kids how to ride at Heartlake Stables. He's a patient teacher.

Dark-blue jeans

All about me

Hair color: Black

Eye color: Brown

Favorite color: Green

Favorite food: Spicy food, milk shakes

Hobbies: Horseback riding, basketball, making movies

Favorite animal: Major, the horse

Horse Show

Every year, Robert and Stephanie organize the Heartlake Horse Show. Robert and Major compete together and Stephanie rides Ruby.

All about me

Hair color: Black

Eye color: Brown

Favorite color: Orange

Favorite food: Vegetable bake, peach cobbler

Hobbies: Reading, art, dog walking, computer games

Favorite animal: Lady (Emma's poodle)

Joanna loves trying new hobbies, from playing computer games or studying animals, to going camping or painting landscapes. She has a vivid imagination and takes her friends on trips to the beach and harbor to look for arty inspiration

> Can't stop! I'm on my way to my art class.

Orange and magenta tank top

Did you know? Joanna is both reliable and dependable— she never misses a shift at the Pet Salon.

Pet passion

Joanna helps out at the Heartlak Pet Salon. She works there with her good friend, Emma. The creative pair like to go to drawing classes together, too.

Sarah

Whether it's a style makeover, a new look for a special occasion, or just a well-deserved pamper session, Sarah can help. She owns Butterfly Beauty Shop and loves making her clients look good and feel fabulous.

Lipstick

Star hair accessory

Style challenge

Sarah admires Emma because she is always updating her look and she's not afraid to try something new. She's her best customer!

Top secret!

Sarah hears all the latest gossip—her customers just seem to relax and tell her things when they are seated in her chair.

Pink sandals

Anna

Olivia's mom, Anna, is a doctor and lives her life at a fast pace. When she's not saving lives in the Emergency Room at Heartlake Hospital, she's keeping fit and active outdoors. Anna's best friend is her younger sister Sophie, the vet.

Hair color: Dark brown

Eye color: Blue

Favorite color: Red

Favorite food: Blueberry pie

Hobbies: Boating, skiing, rock climbing

Favorite animal: Scarlett (Olivia's puppy)

Stylish red pendant

Lilac and silver belt

Kitchen chaos

Anna is a caring mom and a brilliant doctor, but there's one thing she definitely can't do well—cook. She tries her best to cook when she has the time, but the results are often disastrous.

Top secret!

Anna sometimes sneaks to the rooftop patio to get some quiet time away from her busy schedule. It's her favorite spot in the house.

Peter

Olivia and her dad, Peter, have a lot in common. They can both be quiet, serious, and really hardworking. Peter is Editor-in-Chief at the NewsRoom, Heartlake City's buzzing multimedia news center, so he always knows what's happening in the world!

> Breaking news! I've got a great lead on a story.

Family and food

On his days off from work, Peter enjoys cooking for his family on the outdoor grill. He loves chatting to Olivia about her latest project.

Beard

Loosely knotted tie

All about me

Hair color: Red-brown

Eye color: Hazel

Favorite color: Blue

Favorite food: Anything cooked on an outdoor grill

Hobbies: Reading, doing crossword puzzles, gardening

Favorite animal: Kitty (Olivia's cat)

Did you know? Peter is an amazing storyteller. Olivia and her friends love to listen to his tales about the NewsRoom.

Tan shoes

Dr. Sophie

Sophie is the Heartlake City veterinarian, and Olivia's aunt, but everyone else calls her Aunt Sophie, too. She's so caring and kind, and always has time for a chat and a cup of tea.

Green medical cap

Green veterinarian's uniform

All about me

Hair color: Mid-brown

Eye color: Blue

Favorite color: Yellow

Favorite food: Chocolate fondant, s'mores

Hobbies: Baking, hiking, salsa dancing

Favorite animal: All of them!

Pamper time

Busy Sophie was surprised to find that she enjoyed a day at the Shopping Mall spa. She now likes to book a relaxing facial or manicure on her rare days off.

Clean, white shoes

Ms. Stevens

Ms. Maggie Stevens teaches science at Heartlake High and she's passionate about the subject. She's a stickler for the students handing homework in on time, but only because she cares. She wants them to be able to follow their dreams.

Glasses

Top teacher

Ms. Stevens might be strict sometimes, but she's a popular teacher. She inspires her students to do experiments and explore the amazing world of science.

Sensible skirt suit

Top secret!
Ms. Stevens sees great potential in Olivia. She thinks she will be a talented scientist one day.

33

Theresa

Stephanie, Andrea, Mia, Emma, and Olivia all look up to Theresa. She's sophisticated, elegant, and a horseback riding expert. Plus, they always see Theresa hanging out with her friends at the coolest spots in Heartlake City.

Expert advice

Theresa works at the Summer Riding Camp. She is a great teacher because she's passionate about helping others learn all about horses.

All about me

Hair color: Red

Eye color: Hazel

Favorite color: Mint green

Favorite food: Sushi, Thai food

Hobbies: Horseback riding, going to the theater, karaoke

Favorite animal: Foxie, the horse

Stylish cropped riding jacket

Did you know?
Theresa loves all the horses at the Heartlake Stables, but lazy, lovable Foxie is her favorite.

Black riding boots

Marie

Marie inherited the City Park Café from her aunt and has made it one of the most popular hangouts in town. People come from all over to taste her mouthwatering menu and listen to one of Marie's famous stories.

Lemon meringue pie

World traveler

Marie has traveled all around the world, gathering tasty recipe ideas and having amazing adventures. She has many exciting tales to tell.

I've been testing recipes all day.

Marie's work uniform— matching pink shirt and skirt

Top secret!
Marie has traveled the world but she can't fix a coffee machine— Olivia does that for her.

Magenta sandals

Animals

Heartlake City is home to some of the cutest, cuddliest, and cleverest creatures. The girls and their friends love their pets, but they like to care for injured or stray animals they find in the countryside and exotic animals they discover on their exciting jungle adventures, too.

Let's go for a ride in Whispering Woods!

Bella

Mia's horse, Bella, is brilliant at jumping, though she's often a bit nervous—luckily Mia can usually calm her. As soon as she saw the cute chestnut brown foal, Mia fell in love with her. Ever since then, Bella and Mia have been best friends.

Blaze

Top secret!
Mia thinks that she and Bella were destined to be together! Mia's grandmother rode a horse related to Bella.

Happy horse

At first Bella felt nervous in her new home at Heartlake Stables, but Mia made her feel safe. Now, Bella is eight years old and thinks she is the luckiest horse in the world!

Mia brushes Bella's coat to a shiny sheen.

Mia's Top 3
Things to do with Bella

1. Explore the countryside around Heartlake City.

2. Enter jumping competitions.

3. Tell her all her secrets while she grooms her.

Grooming equipment

Maxie

Maxie the cat was rescued by Olivia, Mia, Andrea, Emma, and Stephanie and he now lives outside Olivia's tree house. Friendly Maxie loves to bring the girls gifts—dead mice and other delicacies he found in the trash!

Did you know?
Maxie has one golden rule— no dogs are allowed at the tree house!

Favorite spots

Maxie has three favorite places: The lookout at the top of the tree house because it has a great view, the bales of hay at Heartlake Stables, where he likes to play, and Sunshine Ranch, because he can have a cozy nap on a soft hay bed.

Gray fur with stripes

Hay bale

Maxie's Top 3
Things to do

1. Watch Andrea sing near the City Park Café.

2. Join the girls on their Heartlake City adventures.

3. Hang out with his pal Goldie at the tree house.

Ranch wheelbarrow

Oscar and Jojo

They might be the same species, but these two hedgehogs are total opposites: Oscar is a sophisticated city guy, while Jojo is a country girl who likes eating bugs. There is one thing that they do agree on though—humans are great fun!

Fruit fan

Mia found Oscar behind Heartlake Vet and soon made friends with him. She learned that he loves fruit, but not apples.

Top secret!

Jojo has more than 36 brothers and sisters, so her secret hideaway is a great escape. Only Oscar knows the location!

Jojo's secret hideaway

Fall leaves frame hideaway

Rake for gathering leaves

Oscar

Oscar's uneaten apple

Daisy

Stephanie met Daisy during one of her Pet Patrols in search of missing and injured animals. The rabbit was muddy, lost, and frightened, but Stephanie soon fixed her up. When no one came to claim Daisy, Stephanie adopted her. Now Daisy enjoys co-starring in Mia's magic shows!

Bunny buddies

When Stephanie and her friends have sleepovers, Daisy goes too. Daisy is best friends with Andrea's rabbit, Jazz. They love to munch carrots together.

Magician's top hat

Stage lights

Did you know?
Once, Mia's famous disappearing bunny trick went a bit wrong—Daisy disappeared but she didn't reappear for a whole five minutes!

Daisy's Top 3
Bunny days out

1. Helping Stephanie deliver cupcakes in her convertible.

2. Starring in Mia's famous disappearing bunny trick.

3. Taking a trip to see the animals at Sunshine Ranch.

Ta-da! Daisy reappears!

Magic show purple curtain

41

Goldie

Goldie is a yellow warbler, who lives by Olivia's tree house. She first came to Heartlake City when she hurt her wing. Olivia found her, and Mia nursed her back to health. Goldie liked Heartlake City so much that she decided to stay forever.

Up, up, and away!

Goldie loves to fly around Heartlake City and often visits her friends. She is a curious bird—she likes to keep a lookout at the clubhouse of the Heartlake Flying Club.

Olivia built Goldie this birdhouse.

Goldie's favorite place to perch

Top secret!

Goldie has a beautiful singing voice, but few people have ever heard it, since she's always busily flying off somewhere!

Ladybug

Scarlett

Olivia's puppy, Scarlett, is a sweet, friendly dog. Scarlett's original owner didn't know how to train her and gave her up for adoption. Now Scarlett lives with Olivia and she is very happy. She has lots of fun hanging out with Olivia and her friends, running really fast and chasing balls.

Pup in training

Olivia, Mia, Andrea, Stephanie, and Emma all worked together to train Scarlett. They are currently teaching her how to balance on seesaws and run around cones with a ball. Mia wants to enter her in the Heartlake Dog Show!

Scarlett's Top 3
Games

1. Playing fetch with Olivia.
2. Riding the seesaw with Mia.
3. Joining in with Stephanie's soccer practice.

Scarlett thinks she can play soccer as well as Stephanie!

Long ears

Cone obstacles to run between

Soccer ball

Did you know?
Olivia's Aunt Sophie, the vet, gave Scarlett as a gift to Olivia. She knew Olivia would give Scarlett a good home.

Robin

Robin is the perfect partner for his fashion-conscious owner, Emma. He loves to look elegant and stylish at all times, so he adores being groomed and accessorized. Robin's favorite color is light blue—perhaps it is because it matches his eyes!

Team effort

When Robin first met Emma she was a novice rider, but he helped her to grow in confidence and skill, and now they even enter gymkhana competitions. They just like to have fun, but sometimes they surprise themselves and win!

Top secret!

Robin is working on a unique way of flicking his mane. It'll be his signature pose. Fabulous!

Emma

Winner's ribbon

Water spray

Brush for de-tangling Robin's mane and tail

Bubbles

Ambersands Beach is not just great for sunbathing, it is also home to one of Heartlake City's most famous residents, Bubbles the turtle. He is nearly 80 years old, which is not unusual for a turtle, and he lives beneath a shady palm tree.

Reliable reptile

Bubbles is very wise and visitors to the beach often tell him their problems. When Olivia couldn't master surfing at first, Bubbles listened and nodded his head. She must keep trying!

Palm tree roof

Clamshell contains precious pearl

Did you know?
Bubbles loves to explore the ocean. He once found a clamshell with a pearl inside!

Entrance to Bubbles' oasis

Bubbles' private rock pool

Charlie

Energetic puppy Charlie is sweet and loyal, but most of all he's really goofy and makes everyone laugh. Mia met Charlie at Page's Pets, the animal shelter. As soon as she saw the cute brown patch over his right eye, Mia fell in love.

Faithful friend

Charlie likes to follow Mia everywhere, but his favorite place is Heartlake Stables. When Mia rides Bella, Charlie runs along beside them.

Woof woof!

Charlie's puppy house

Top secret!

Charlie is a good puppy, but he has one weakness—rabbits. As soon as he gets a whiff of one, he just has to chase it.

Charlie is waiting for his next adventure.

Juliet

Orangutan Juliet loves exploring her jungle habitat. Her long arms are ideal for swinging from vine to vine and she knows just where to find the biggest bananas. If you listen carefully, you may also hear her call!

Jungle vine

Juliet stashes her fruity snacks here.

Going ape

Emma is Juliet's favorite person. While snacking on termites, hungry Juliet got trapped in a cave by a rockfall. Brave Emma dug her out.

Did you know?
Orangutans live in trees. Every night, Juliet builds a comfortable nest from branches, twigs, and leaves.

Jazz

Bouncy Jazz is a bundle of energy—a great match for his owner, Andrea! Mia introduced Andrea to a litter of baby bunnies she was caring for at Heartlake Vet, and Andrea was instantly smitten. She chose the most active rabbit and named him Jazz.

Home sweet home

Jazz's hutch has an indoor shelter and an outdoor play area. Andrea makes sure her pet always has lots of water to drink and carrots to eat

Do you want to hear my new song, Jazz?

Andrea's Top 3
Jazz Facts

1. He's super friendly and loves to be cuddled.

2. He likes to chew cardboard.

3. He is best friends with Stephanie's rabbit, Daisy.

Broom for keeping Jazz's hutch tidy

Pail of water for cleaning the hutch

Did you know?
Andrea hopes that her parents will allow her to get a dog or a cat someday, too.

Jazz

Misty

Misty is a cute baby deer who lives on the edge of Whispering Woods. She enjoys basking in the warm sunshine, swimming in the river, and playing tag with her brother and sister.

Snack time

Misty's mom taught her how to forage in the woods. Misty likes tasty wild berries and fresh grass the most.

Misty's tree home

White spots show that Misty is young.

Top secret!

Misty lives in the woods with her mom, brother, and sister. Her mom munches the flowers in the city—no one's quick enough to catch her!

Wild mushroom

Blu

Blu the baby bear lives in a cave next to a river. It's the perfect place for a bear who likes to spend time alone. What's more, the river is packed with his favorite food—fish. Blu is a growing bear, with a big appetite!

Broken bridge

Blu wanted to cross the bridge over the river to eat some juicy berries, but the wooden planks were rotten. Fortunately, Mia and Matthew were able to rescue him.

Did you know?
Blu is a species known as a black bear, but black bears can actually be black, brown, white, and other colors.

Blu's cave home

Milo
and Sheen

Dolphins Milo and Sheen made friends with Mia when she was exploring the ocean on the *Dolphin Cruiser.* Mia was fascinated by the playful brother and sister, especially the way they "talk" to each other by whistling, clicking, and squeaking.

Dolphin Cruiser

Milo, the brother

Sheen, the sister

Showing off

Milo and Sheen perform tricks for Mia and her friends Andrew and Maya. They jump out of the water, ride waves, and catch fish that the friends throw to them.

Top secret!

Milo and Sheen like to play pranks on other animals. It's fun to scare pelicans or tease turtles!

Hazel

Hungry Hazel is obsessed with finding nuts and seeds. Andrea even caught the cheeky squirrel foraging in her trash! However, she decided that Hazel was the cutest garbage thief she'd ever met and hopes they can become friends.

Tree house home

Hazel

Getting closer

At first, Hazel was a little shy around Andrea, but Andrea found the perfect way to Hazel's heart—a basket of crunchy acorns.

Retractable ladder

Did you know?

Olivia is thinking up ways to squirrel-proof Andrea's family's trash cans.

Java

Motor-mouth macaw, Java, was brought to the Jungle Rescue Base after she was found hurt under some leaves. The girls built this feisty bird a perch near the watering fountain. Java can mimic anything people say, so it's best not to tell her any secrets!

Bird's-eye view

Java has a very important job at the Base—she's the lookout on top of the watchtower. Whenever visitors arrive, she squawks loudly to let everyone know.

Top secret!

Java has recently laid some eggs. Stephanie found them and is determined to keep them safe. Will Java be a mom soon?

Java adores eating tasty berries.

Java's special perch

Coco

Boisterous puppy Coco spends most days with Stephanie because his owner works long hours at the Heartlake Robot Lab. Coco loves having adventures with Stephanie, but his favorites always seem to involve getting them both wet!

Puppy pals

Coco's best friend is Celie, Marie's dog. When the two pooches finish playing in the park, they always head back to Marie's City Park Café to sniff out some tasty leftovers.

> You look much tidier now, Coco!

Stephanie's dog grooming brush

Coco's Top 3
Things to do with Stephanie

1. Jog around Lake Heart (and bark "Hi" to Celie).

2. Jump in the lake, get out, and shake his coat.

3. Dig up dropped key rings and other dogs' bones!

Cute black nose

Pink bow

Top secret!

Stephanie treats Coco as if he is her dog. Her mom won't let her have a dog because she doesn't want muddy pawprints in the house!

Clara

Sunshine Ranch is never quiet, thanks to Clara the hen. She's always clucking about something—whether it's the fact that she's just broken her own egg-laying record (three in a single day!) or letting everyone know that there's a fox on the loose.

Yard gossip

When Clara isn't laying eggs, she likes to catch up on all the Ranch gossip. She always drops by Cream's hutch when Daisy comes from the city to stay.

Did you know?
Silly Clara often stops the farm traffic by standing in the middle of the road!

Clara's favorite spot to perch

Entrance to the chicken coop

Mia collects freshly laid eggs

Major and Ruby

At first glance quiet, sensible Major and noisy, mischievous Ruby might not seem like a perfect match, but they're best friends. Both horses are talented jumpers and they often travel to shows together. They don't mind who wins!

Special bond

Robert loves riding Major and treats him like a special family member. Andrea likes Major, too—and he loves her singing!

Major's tail bow

Ruby's purple saddle

White blaze

Second prize ribbon

Top secret!
Ruby can be a little stubborn, but Stephanie keeps her sweet with her special oat cookies.

56

Jewel

Emma first met Jewel at the Pet Salon, and when she heard that the cute cat needed a new family, she couldn't wait to adopt her. Jewel is a fun-loving feline who likes to explore. Emma put a bell on Jewel's collar so that she won't get lost—it looks stylish, too!

Did you know?
Jewel is very loving. When she really likes someone she rubs up against their legs.

Jewel, that collar is so you!

Poodle pal

Jewel felt shy when she first got to Emma's house, but Emma's dog, Lady, made her feel welcome. Now, they sleep curled up in the same bed.

Pink ears

Blue collar with bell inside heart pendant

Gray paws

57

Kiki

Kiki the parrot spends a few months of the year at Heartlake High. The busy bird flies from class to class, learning new words and making the students laugh. Sociable Kiki is great fun to have around!

Canopy over perch

Bright green plumage

Moat feature is also a drinking bowl

Did you know?
When she's not visiting Heartlake High, Kiki lives at a zoo near Heartlake City.

Lunch pal

Kiki sometimes perches on the bench near Matthew. She likes to have lunch with him—she takes sneaky bites from his juicy green apple!

Celie

Life couldn't get better for Marie's dog, Celie the poodle. She spends the day hanging out on the patio of the City Park Café and playing with her pals at Lake Heart before returning to the Café for a nap. She snores so loudly that it makes the customers giggle!

Pampered poodle

Marie is Celie's favorite person. She's so kind and loving—and she makes great pies! Celie's pooch pals are Coco and Lady. Lady is also Celie's cousin.

Top secret!

Celie and Lady look so alike that sometimes they swap places. The only way to tell them apart is the color of their eyes!

Celie has green eyes. Her cousin, Lady, has blue eyes.

New hairstyle created by Emma

Dog grooming brush

Celie's Top 3
Pooch pastimes

1. Trying Marie's latest pie flavors

2. Taking a swim in Lake Heart with Coco

3. Getting a top-to-toe makeover from Emma

Kitty

When Olivia and her family moved to Heartlake City, their nine-year-old cat, Kitty, came too. Kitty misses her old pals, but she loves to play with Olivia's new friends, especially cat lovers Mia and Emma.

Special spot

Kitty is a house cat, which means she doesn't go outside. Instead, she sits on the sunny window seat, all day long, watching the world go by.

Top secret!

Maxie, the stray cat, wants to play with Kitty, but he does not feel confident enough to go inside the house. Instead, the two cats look at each other through the window.

It's time for your catnap, Kitty.

Fluffy tail

Olivia's cozy bed

Bobbi

Branches help Bobbi hide and provide shade.

Bobbi the lion cub lives with her family by a watering hole on the grassy savanna. She is the youngest member of the pride so she is too small to hunt with her mom or patrol with her dad. Bobbi loves rolling about and playing with her brothers, instead.

Safe and sound

When the girls found Bobbi all alone, they thought she needed rescuing. But Mia knew better—her family would be back soon. Bobbi sometimes visits her new friends at the Jungle Tree Sanctuary.

Did you know?
A group of lions that live together is known as a pride. Bobbi has many friends in the pride.

Watering hole

Foxie and Champion

It's not just the people who look forward to Summer Riding Camp, the horses love it, too. Foxie and his sister Champion like taking their new friends on adventurous trail rides or over exciting water jumps.

Horse care

Champion always stands patiently while Emma and Stephanie groom her. Her favorite reward for good behavior is usually a crunchy carrot!

Champion

Foxie

Did you know?
Champion is 11 years old and she used to be a race horse. Foxie is 15 years old.

Foxie loves juicy apples.

Tony

Tony the jungle chameleon is an
interesting reptile to have around.
He can flick his long tongue to catch
bugs, change his skin color to act as
camouflage, and also swivel his eyes to
see all around without moving his head!

Secret stowaway

Once, when Stephanie was busy
steering the Jungle Rescue Base's
boat, Tony climbed aboard.
Now he often joins the girls
on their rescue missions—of
course, he tries to blend right in!

Andrea and Tony
explore the dense
jungle with a lamp.

Tony's tail is
changing
color.

Cream

Like all the animals on Sunshine Ranch, Cream the angora rabbit has a job to do: Every three months, Cream's coat is sheared to make wool. Thanks to Cream, Mia and her friends all have stylish knitted scarves!

Farm friends

Cream's best friends are Clara the hen and horses Mocca and Fame. Mia and Liza often visit, too, bringing Maxie the cat and Daisy the rabbit.

Top secret!
Naughty Cream and Daisy like to nibble on the carrots and lettuces in Liza's vegetable garden.

Cream

Stephanie's rabbit, Daisy

Liza

Hay

Sunshine and Snow

Sunshine was adopted by the Summer Riding Camp when her owner became too old to care for her. Everyone loves sweet, gentle Sunshine, especially Olivia. One day, Sunshine surprised everyone by giving birth to a tiny foal, Snow.

Special day

Everyone is excited about the arrival of Snow. Olivia is even creating a "foal-cam" to capture Snow's progress, while Emma is taking lots of pictures.

Sunshine's bridle

Snow's bow decoration

Long, skinny legs

Did you know?
Olivia delivered Sunshine's foal all by herself! When she saw that the foal was white, Olivia named her Snow.

Bamboo

Shy baby panda Bamboo was separated from his parents and hurt by another animal. Luckily, a woman from a nearby village found him and took him to the Jungle Rescue Base, where the girls are looking after him. Bamboo is safe and sound there.

Jungle teacher

Pandas need to know how to climb trees. Most are taught by their parents, but Bamboo has a special teacher at the Base—Romeo the monkey.

Did you know?
The aim of the Jungle Rescue Base is to release animals like Bamboo back into the wild when they are ready.

Bamboo's hideaway has a fallen branch to crawl across.

Slide

Hoo

Most tawny owls live in forests but Hoo lives in Ms. Stevens' science classroom at Heartlake High. The curious bird always wakes up at dismissal to perch on the window ledge and watch the students go home.

Teaching assistant

Owls are nocturnal, but Hoo makes a special effort to stay awake to watch Ms. Stevens teach her biology lessons. She sits on her perch by the telescope.

Twit twoo!

Beak

Top secret!

Olivia, Joanna, and Emma are hoping to train Hoo to carry secret messages.

Ms. Stevens

Lighter brown plumage on chest

Ms. Stevens' Top 3
Owl Facts

1. Owls eat rodents, such as mice.

2. A group of owls is known as a parliament.

3. Owls can turn their heads 270 degrees.

Plum

Plum is a young turtle who lives in a watering hole near Jungle Falls. Her home has a shady palm tree, a beautiful waterfall, and as many crayfish and fruit as she can eat. What more could a water-loving, greedy turtle need?

Surprise visitor

Plum sometimes steals food from the pantry of the Jungle Rescue Base. She is a sneaky little turtle!

Did you know?
Plum loves to take a (slow) walk under the light of a full moon.

Leafy palm tree

Waterfall flows down rocks

Berries

Casper

Adventurous Casper lives on the shores of Antarctica, near the South Pole. This friendly Emperor Penguin charms his brothers and sisters into joining him on intrepid adventures, but they often struggle to find their way home!

Fish food
Casper likes to eat fish three times a day. Luckily for him, there is a constant supply in Antarctica.

Black and white feathers

Casper's home has an awesome water slide to zoom down.

Top secret!
Casper's siblings work together to find their way home, but Casper likes to think it's down to his tracking skills!

Cozy bed tucked away behind slide

Biscuit

Olivia, Andrea, Emma, Stephanie, and Mia came across this cute bear cub in the jungle. They were a little scared of him at first, but soon realised he is friendly, almost tame, and a bit of a show-off! Biscuit spends his days fishing, digging, and climbing trees.

Happy home

Biscuit sleeps in his cozy cave all winter, and doesn't wake up until spring. After such a long sleep, he's ready to have some fun, and a fresh fish or two for dinner.

Shaggy brown fur

Wet black nose

Top secret!
The girls are a bit embarrassed that they tried to "rescue" Biscuit. He was perfectly fine—just having a snooze!

Huge paws

Satin

Seal pup Satin lives in Antarctica near her penguin pal Casper. She spends her days diving under the ice to catch fish or playing games with her seal friends. It's cold and icy in Antarctica, but Satin has a thick layer of blubber to keep her warm.

Playtime!

Satin's favorite pastime is sliding. When she isn't climbing up and sliding down huge icy hills, she's practicing tricks on her very own seesaw.

Orange ball

Satin's rocky home

Did you know?
Satin has great hearing and a really loud call. Her friends can even hear her when she's swimming under the ice!

Lady

Emma's pet poodle is aptly named: Lady is elegant, well-mannered, and always perfectly groomed. She might act a little superior sometimes, but Lady is really very kind, especially to her best friends, Celie and Jewel.

Fashion advice

Emma takes Lady when she goes to the Mall. The stylish pooch is always curious to see the latest fashions.

Top secret!
Lady lets Emma try out the latest poodle fashion designs on her, but she has her limits! Sometimes she just walks away.

Dog shampoo

Long curly ears

Pink collar with silver bone accessory

Flame

Olivia rescued this cute baby tiger near the waterfall when he was hiking in the jungle. The curious cub had been exploring and got stuck. Flame was so glad to see Olivia and it seems that they are becoming friends—Flame loves people.

River rescue

When Olivia saw Flame heading toward a waterfall, she fixed a dam to stop the waterfall's flow. She then safely pulled Flame to the riverbank.

Did you know?

Olivia and the girls like to make up stories about Flame. They've even created a legend about her!

Olivia and the girls built this special temple for Flame.

Jungle ferns

Orange fur with black stripes

Felix

Lively Felix is another animal whose life changed when he met Mia. She adopted him after she found him meowing forlornly in City Park. Noisy Felix hasn't stopped meowing since, but now it's because he's really happy!

Perfect pals

Charlie wasn't sure about Felix at first, he's noisy, and he's a CAT. But they have one important thing in common—Mia—and now they are best friends.

Scratching post

Three-story playhouse

Did you know?
Emma designed Felix's playhouse and Olivia built it. It's located on Mia's front porch.

Fish snack

Ramp for easy access

Niki

The other horses at Heartlake Stables look up to Niki. Not only is he the biggest horse at the Stables, but he's also the bossiest. The dark brown stallion acts as though the other horses could learn a lot from him!

Perfect pair

Niki is usually ridden by Katharina, and he couldn't wish for a better partner. She is as energetic and talented as he is! Together they teach the other horses and riders how to jump high and gallop fast.

Top secret!
Sometimes Niki secretly splashes in puddles when the other horses aren't looking!

You did a great job today, Niki—have a tasty carrot.

Pink saddle

Katharina holds Niki's favorite snack.

White jodhpurs don't stay spotless for long!

Romeo

People can't help loving this mischievous monkey! Romeo is a jungle clown and doesn't mean to cause trouble, he just likes to have fun. He's much-loved at the Jungle Rescue Base—only Java the macaw is annoyed by him.

Monkeying around

Romeo keeps stealing the girls' things from the Base's living quarters. Emma and Olivia have a great idea to build a fun play structure, to keep Romeo and the other monkeys out of trouble!

Medicine jar

Romeo's Top 3
Pranks and jokes

1. Hiding Java's seeds and fruit

2. Riding the medicine cart at top speed

3. Doing impressions of all the other animals

Top secret!

Whenever the medicine cart goes missing, Romeo the rascal is usually to blame. He loves taking the cart for rides.

Stethoscope

Medical chart

Lucky

Emma often visits the Heartlake Aftercare Center to play with the animals and kids. When Emma first met Lucky, the bunny was recovering from a broken foot. Now her foot has healed, Emma is teaching her some tricks. Lucky loves to perform!

New home

Emma and her friends built Lucky a fancy new hutch. It also has a vegetable garden filled with delicacies. She is the happiest rabbit in Heartlake City.

Did you know?
Lucky used to raid the neighbor's vegetable garden, but now she has one of her own.

Long, gray fur

Balance beam

Ramp

Max

Adorable pup, Max, is staying at Page's Pets, the animal shelter. When he's not gnawing on juicy bones, Max loves to practice his agility on seesaws and slides. He's a smart, active pup and hopes to be adopted soon.

Temporary home

Max is happy at Page's Pets, but what he really needs is a new family to love. Andrea wants to take him home, but she just needs to convince her parents...

Seesaw

Blue bow

Bone

Top secret!
Andrea isn't the only one who is interested in Max—Matthew would like to adopt him, too!

Page's Pets Top 3
Animal shelter rules

1. Every animal is welcome.

2. Animals in need will be fed and given a clean, warm bed.

3. Rescued animals will be given to kind families.

Fame, Blaize, and Mocca

These happy horses all live on Sunshine Ranch. Mocca, a curious brown farm horse, was born on the Ranch. Ultra-white Blaize came here as Mia's first horse. He is the leader of the Ranch animals. Cute foal Fame is a brand new addition to Blaize and Mocca's family.

Happy event

Animal expert Mia helped Mocca to give birth to Fame! She loves taking care of the happy horse family. She makes sure they have plenty of fresh hay.

Did you know?
Mocca is the strongest horse on Sunshine Ranch. Every winter, Mocca pulls the Sunshine Ranch snow sled.

Mocca is saddled up and ready for a ride.

Mia is grooming Blaize.

Fame

Cotton

Cotton the lamb is another new arrival at Sunshine Ranch. He is in good hands: Super-organized Stephanie helped to deliver him and she knows just how to care for him. She takes time bathing him and combing his woolly coat.

Did you know?
Cotton is best friends with Fame the Foal. They run and jump together in the fields.

Loving care

Stephanie feeds Cotton with special bottles of warm milk. She loves looking after him, and she already has big plans—she wants to enter him into Heartlake's annual Farm Show.

Bottle of milk

Soft, woolly coat

Zip

This curious frog likes to take risks. So, when he spies Olivia steering her boat through the murky jungle waters, he leaps aboard. Zip's noisy calls and trills help her guide the boat and even warn her about any crocodiles ahead!

ungle explorer

ip loves hopping around the ungle looking for exciting ventures. As an amphibian e can live on land or water, he's up for anything!

Olivia uses a lever to steer.

Single-person speedboat

Top secret!

Zip can be a bit nosy—his long neck is good for spying through the leaves. He saw all of Blu's rope bridge rescue from start to finish!

Zip takes a rest on a lily pad.

Hobbies

Andrea, Emma, Mia, Olivia, Stephanie, and their friends are always busy. They already have so many cool hobbies, from soccer and skateboarding, to music and designing, but there's always time to learn something new!

I've got a great idea for a song.

Music

Andrea loves to take center stage and perform for her friends. They always give her their honest critique: She's a superstar! However, Andrea isn't the only person in Heartlake City with musical talent—the girls are thinking of starting a band.

Girl band

Mia is teaching herself the drums, Olivia plays the keyboard, and Stephanie is taking electric guitar lessons.

Top secret!

Stephanie has kept her guitar lessons a secret from everyone! But now she feels ready to perform in front of her friends.

Andrea's name in lights

Stephanie's electric guitar

Speakers

Andrea's Top 3
Superstar tips

1. Practice every day.
2. Be original and create your own sound.
3. Own the stage—performance is everything.

Microphone stand

Magic

One summer, Mia discovered a talent for magic—it started with a card trick and now she baffles the other girls with all kinds of illusions. Olivia helped build a cabinet and curtains for Mia's set, and now Mia is ready to enter the Heartlake City Magic Show!

Abracadabra!

Of course, Mia's best trick involves an animal. With a wave of her wand, she can make Stephanie's bunny, Daisy, disappear!

Magic cabinet

And now for my next trick...

Playing cards

Mia's Top 3
Magic tricks

1. Making a bunny disappear and reappear.

2. Turning one flower into a whole bunch.

3. Knowing which card has been picked from the deck.

Fancy magician's tuxedo

Dance

Andrea and Stephanie love to dance and have both been dancing since they were very young. Andrea has a natural talent for choreography, while Stephanie specializes in jazz and performs in school shows.

Rehearsal

Before a show, Andrea makes sure she looks perfect, and then rehearses her dance steps. She doesn't want to put a foot wrong

Top secret!

Andrea tried to teach Olivia how to dance, but it was hopeless! Olivia prefers science to samba.

Andrea's Top 3
Dance ambitions

1. To choreograph a dance for Stephanie

2. To teach young kids how to dance

3. To invent her own dance fitness craze

Spotlights

Gold tiara

Practice makes perfect.

Makeup table

Ballet barre

Designing

Emma spends so much time working on her designs that she has her own design studio in her house. It's a great place to create costumes for the school musical, photograph her work, or plan her redesign of Mia's bedroom.

Creative tools

Emma often uses a computer to visualize her ideas, but she is a talented artist so she sometimes prefers a pencil!

Emma's Top 3
Design projects

1. Making pebble jewelry with kindergartners

2. Entering the Teen Fashion Design contest

3. Creating a new design web show, called "Together We Design"

Messy drawers

Mood board

Camera

Design table

Did you know?
Emma recently taught herself how to knit, and knitted woolly hats for her friends.

Inventing

Olivia's brain is always buzzing with clever ideas. She has her own workshop where she invents cool gadgets, creates smart apps, and recycles old junk into something fabulous. Olivia has even built a robot—Zobo.

Special formula

First, Olivia uses her science know-how to plan a new invention. Then, she uses her tools to create a prototype.

Top secret!

Olivia wants to program Zobo to play soccer for a new robot sports event. She's still in the early stages of planning!

Microscope

Chemicals

Power tools

Remote control pad

Zobo

Zobo's Top 3
Robot skills

1. Using a sound sensor to find birds in the trees by Olivia's tree house

2. Projecting TV shows and movies anywhere

3. Clearing weeds from overgrown paths

Karate

Sometimes Emma likes to take time out from designing and creating fabulous things. Karate is great for feeling powerful, and for learning to focus the body and mind in new ways.

Trophies
Emma admires the trophies at the dojo. The older children have won many trophies!

Did you know?
Emma has a black belt in karate. This means she is at the highest level.

Dojo entrance

忍者

Wow! That was hard.

Water cooler

Helmet

Emma's Top 3
Karate Facts

1. Karate originated in Japan.

2. "Karate" means "empty hand" in Japanese.

3. Karate lessons take place in a dojo.

Chopping block

Soccer

Stephanie has been playing soccer ever since she learned to walk. She loves being part of a team, and she's especially good at calling the plays and getting the team to work together. She's a playmaker and a striker, and practices shooting every day.

Training session

Stephanie jogs and eats healthy snacks to keep her body in peak condition. Being fit helps her to improve her soccer skills.

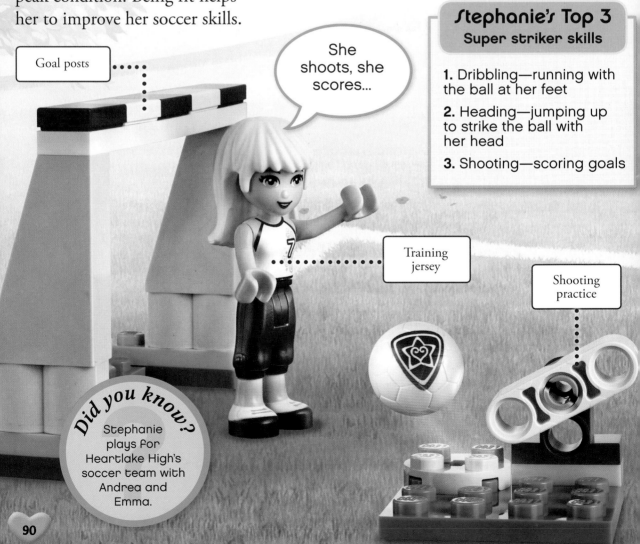

Goal posts

She shoots, she scores...

Stephanie's Top 3
Super striker skills

1. Dribbling—running with the ball at her feet
2. Heading—jumping up to strike the ball with her head
3. Shooting—scoring goals

Training jersey

Shooting practice

Did you know?
Stephanie plays for Heartlake High's soccer team with Andrea and Emma.

The Great Outdoors

From the Clearspring Mountains and the Whispering Woods, to Heartlake Farms and Clover Meadows, the countryside around Heartlake City is truly beautiful and the girls love exploring it.

Field work

Olivia often swaps gadgets for gardening at Sunshine Ranch. Well, gardening is biology so it's a science project, too!

Top secret!

When Andrea wants to be alone to write music, she hikes up to her hut in the Clearspring Mountains. It's so peaceful there.

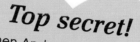

Mountain hut

Andrea's Top 3
Things about being outdoors

1. The amazing scenery inspires her lyrics.

2. Fresh air is great for her voice.

3. In the mountains she can sing as loudly as she likes.

Map

Camera for taking photos of wildlife

Cozy bed

91

Charity Work

Olivia, Emma, Stephanie, Mia, and Andrea are healthy and happy, and they all live in an amazing city. The girls know they are very lucky, so each of them has decided to spend some of their free time helping others.

Making it happen

Andrea uses her blogging and social networking skills to spread the word about all the girls' charity events.

Did you know? Mia is raising money by selling fresh, homemade lemonade. All her profits will go to Page's Pets.

LEMONADE

Emma designed the banner

Lemon juicer

Mia drives to the stand on her mint-green scooter.

100

Mia also sells cookies

Top 3
Fundraising ideas

1. Olivia thinks a sponsored math challenge would be fun.

2. Stephanie is organizing a spectacular bake-off.

3. Emma suggests a fabulous fashion show.

Horseback Riding

Mia, Emma, and Stephanie are all crazy about horses. They love riding them, grooming them, and feeding them. They are even happy to clean their stables, which is known as "mucking out"—it can get more than a little messy!

Out on the trail

The countryside around Heartlake City is perfect for horseback riding. Best friends Ella and Katharina often take their horses Sunshine and Niki for a gallop through Whispering Woods at the weekend.

Riding helmet

Top secret!

Stephanie really wants to win the Heartlake Horse Show. She has been practicing every day with Ruby.

Stephanie's Top 3
Amazing horse facts

1. A horse can sleep lying down or standing up.

2. A baby horse (foal) can trot just after it's born.

3. The fastest horses can gallop at 55 mph (88 km/h).

Horse jump

Caring for Animals

Everyone knows that Mia is an animal lover. In fact, her friends sometimes joke that she prefers animals to people! But Mia isn't the only one who likes animals, her friends all have special pets to look after or creatures to care for.

Hedgehog helper

Emma and her friends take care of Oscar. Emma researched the best food to give hedgehogs—meaty dog food! Oscar adores Emma and her friends. He once followed them to Riding Camp!

Top secret!
Charlie performed so well at the Heartlake Dog Show that Mia is already training him for next year's show.

Bone treat

Mia's Top 3
Dream animal jobs

1. Veterinarian—just like Aunt Sophie

2. Animal psychologist—someone who understands animal behavior

3. Animal shelter worker—somewhere like Page's Pets

Winners' ribbon

Charlie

Cooking

Stephanie is an amazing baker. She is known as the queen of cupcakes! Her friends are less confident in the kitchen, although they like to give cooking a go. Andrea has picked up some tips from working at the City Park Café and Olivia likes to invent new flavor combinations.

Did you know? Stephanie bakes for animals, too. She makes healthy cupcakes and cookies for horses and dogs.

Outdoor cook

Marie, Andrea's boss at the café, has given Andrea some great outdoor cooking advice. Andrea is a little nervous, but her toasted marshmallows are delicious!

Chocolate cake with white frosting

Chocolate, strawberry, and vanilla slice

Outdoor oven

Stephanie's Top 3
Cupcake recipes

1. Totally tempting toffee cupcakes

2. Sensational strawberry shortcake cupcakes

3. Special carrot cupcakes for horses and dogs

Skateboarding

Mia enjoys spending time outdoors, whether it's hiking, mountain biking, or horseback riding. Her newest hobby is skateboarding. She's only just started, but she's working hard to learn tricks. She hopes a skate park will be built in the city one day.

Mia's Top 3
Tricks and Flips

1. Ollie—jumping in the air with the skateboard.

2. Rock and roll—riding to the very top of a ramp and back down.

3. Kickflip—jumping in the air and spinning the board.

Top secret!

The first time Mia skateboarded she fell off. Her friend Matthew helped her get straight back on again and she soon found her balance.

Ice-cream sundae

Cropped pants

Blue skateboard

Out and about

Skateboarding is a great way to travel. Mia often grabs her board and heads out for the day. She likes to pack a picnic—skateboarding gives her a big appetite!

96

Winter Fun

Winter transforms Heartlake City into a beautiful snowy paradise. Stephanie, Mia, Andrea, Olivia, and Emma love this time of year—they can ski, ice-skate, go sledding, or just get cozy with a cup of hot chocolate.

Did you know?
The girls sometimes go snowboarding and skiing at a cool resort, up in the mountains.

Top 3
Things to do in winter

1. Snowshoe all around Heartlake City.
2. Form an ice hockey team.
3. Learn to drive a snowmobile.

Snow fun

Olivia uses science logic, building know-how, and some handy twigs to create wondrous snowpeople. Mia donates her magician's top hat to complete the look.

Mia and Emma love skiing.

Warm scarf

Skate star Lily gives Stephanie some tips.

97

Off to the Beach

There are plenty of fun things to do at Ambersands Beach: Olivia and Andrea build sandcastles, while Stephanie plays soccer and relaxes with her book. Mia enjoys snorkeling and searching the rock pools for sea creatures.

Saving lives

Emma has a part-time job a a junior lifegua at the beach. She helps the lifeguards to kee everyone safe.

Andrea looks for pirate ships through her telescope.

It's a masterpiece!

Seashells

Spade

Sandcastle with pink flag

Top secret!

Olivia loves building sandcastles. Her top tip for building a strong castle is to mix sand and water in a bucket first.

Top 3
Beach rules

1. Don't leave litter on the beach.

2. Don't swim too far out into the ocean.

3. Have fun and come back soon!

Jungle Adventures

Mia, Stephanie, Olivia, Emma, and Andrea love new challenges. So, when Dr. Sophie asked them to help her rescue endangered jungle animals, they all said yes! They couldn't wait to head off on an amazing adventure.

Did you know?
On their second day in the jungle, Dr. Sophie was called to an emergency on a neighboring reserve, leaving the girls and Matthew in charge!

Top 3
Tropical tips

1. Always wear sunscreen.
2. Pack plenty of bug spray.
3. Treat the jungle animals with respect and kindness.

Tony the chameleon

Jungle Falls

Olivia's rescue life buoy

Flame the tiger cub

Jungle team

The girls and their friend Matthew have lots to do in the jungle. There are animals to be rescued, habitats to be repaired, and dangerous areas to be patrolled.

99

Locations

Take a tour of the most important locations in Heartlake City—well according to Stephanie, Mia, Emma, Andrea, and Olivia, at least. You might not find them in every travel guide book, but these are the special places where the girls study, work, have fun, or just like to hang out.

I love staying at Sunshine Ranch.

Heartlake City

Heartlake City is buzzing with fabulous things to do and amazing places to visit: If you want an outdoor adventure, head to the Clearspring Falls or Ambersands Beach. If you like horseback riding, head to Heartlake Stables and the woods surrounding it. Splash around at Heartlake City Pool or grab a bite to eat at Downtown Bakery. Life is never dull in Heartlake City!

Butterfly Beauty Shop

Downtown Bakery

Heartlake Pet Salon

Clearspring Falls

Andrea's House

City Park Café

Lake Heart

Rehearsal Stage

Olivia's House

Heartlake Stables

Olivia's Tree House

Sunshine Ranch

Heartlake Vet

Downtown
Business District

ArtsTown
District

Heartlake
High

Heartlake
Juice Bar

Marina

Heartlake
City Pool

Ambersands
Beach

Stephanie's
Beach House

Heartlake
Lighthouse

103

Happy family

There is always plenty going on at Olivia's house: Olivia's mom is making dinner, Olivia is writing her diary, and Olivia's dad is busy too—relaxing!

Movie night

Olivia and her parents like to sit back and watch movies together. Olivia's favorites are science fiction movies.

Olivia's cat, Kitty, lives here, too.

Olivia's dad cooks on the outdoor grill.

Dinner's ready, Olivia.

Swing time

When Olivia needs a quiet place to think, she heads to her outdoor swing.

Lawnmower

Olivia's House

There's no place like home, especially when it's as fabulous as Olivia's house. Olivia lives at Number 30, Heartlake Heights, with her mom, Anna, and her dad, Peter. Her friends often hang out here, too.

Rooftop patio

It smells amazing, Dad!

Did you know?
Olivia thinks her room is great—it has a balcony wih pretty views and a desk for her laptop and journals.

Vegetable garden

105

Olivia's Tree House

When Olivia and her friends want to chill out by themselves, they head to their own private tree house. Here, they can catch up on the latest news, tell each other secrets, and plan their next adventure.

Stargazing

During the summer, Olivia and her friends often have sleepovers in the tree house. Olivia fixed up this telescope so they can study the stars together.

Secret hangout

Olivia found the tree house in her backyard. Emma, Mia, Stephanie, and Andrea helped her to fix it up. The ladder is the only way to get inside.

Stray cat Maxie has his own bed at the tree house.

Safe place

The tree house is the perfect place to hide the girls' treasures. This secret box is cleverly concealed underneath some leaves.

Lookout post

I can see the ocean from up here!

Steps

Top secret!
At the tree house, the girls add to their special scrapbook with stories of their friendship and adventures.

Red Oak tree

Secret treasure box

Heartlake High

Heartlake High is a friendly, happy place to learn. Ms. Stevens and her fellow teachers aim to challenge and inspire all the students at the school. They want to help every girl and boy reach their full potential, whatever that might be.

School lockers

The pupils have lockers to store their books. Someone has put a letter in Stephanie's locker. They want her to run for school president!

The school's pet owl, Hoo

Bathroom

Did you know?
There are incredible views of the ocean from Heartlake High's classrooms.

HIG
SCHO

Getting creative

At Heartlake High, students are encouraged to try new subjects. Stephanie thought that art was Emma's thing, not hers. Now she thinks she might have a new hobby!

Science class

Matthew usually prefers skateboarding to science, but this microscope has got his interest. It shows him things super close-up. That's cool!

Science lab

Music studio

Time to go home! See you tomorrow.

HLC

Ms. Stevens

Outside picnic area

City Park Café

Everyone knows where to go to get the tastiest pies, the frothiest milk shakes, and the yummiest fruit salads—the City Park Café. Located right by Lake Heart, it's the perfect spot to meet friends and enjoy Marie's delicious, homecooked food.

Marie turns off the bright lights when she shuts the Café for the day.

Busy day
Marie works hard all day at the City Park Café, baking, waiting tables, and washing the dirty dishes.

This new strawberry milk shake recipe is your best yet!

Cupcakes are one of Marie's specialties.

Cleaning up

Marie likes the Café to look welcoming. Every night she sweeps the floor, wipes the tables, and leaves everything spotlessly clean.

Teamwork

Luckily, Marie has a helper —Andrea. Andrea loves her part-time job at the Café, especially when Marie lets her sing for the customers!

A batch of freshly baked cupcakes

Marie's broom

Top secret!

Sometimes Marie has to ring the bell on the counter, just to remind her chatty waitress, Andrea, that there is food to be served!

Candy dispenser

Stylish ride

Traveling to and from Riding Camp is fun. Stephanie drives while Emma and Ella chat. The girls have so much luggage that they need a trailer!

Summer Riding Camp

Stephanie and Emma love coming to Summer Riding Camp. They can spend all day horseback riding, feeding and grooming the horses, and hanging out with their friend Ella, and Theresa, the riding instructor.

Top secret!

Emma and Stephanie share a bedroom when they stay at Camp. They always secretly organize a midnight feast!

Stables

Sunshine

Practice ring

Theresa is the camp's riding instructor and head counselor. She is teaching Emma and Stephanie how to drive a horse and trap. It's not easy, but it's a lot of fun!

Camp fire

After an energetic day on horseback, the girls relax by toasting marshmallows on the camp fire and telling each other stories.

Spare saddles

Spare bridles

Foxie

Champion

Downtown Bakery

Downtown Bakery sells a mouthwatering range of international cakes, cookies, breads, and pastries. Customers line up around the block for their favorite treats!

New assistant
The Bakery is owned by the parents of Mia's friend, Danielle. Danielle has got Mia a part-time job here.

Freshly baked bread and cookies

A lot to learn
Mia has more experience of pets than pastries but she's willing to learn. So, what's this thing for again?

Outdoor cake stand

Top secret!
No one knows the Downtown Bakery's special recipe for French pastries. It has a secret ingredient —honey!

Oven

Fire extinguisher ready for Mia's next visit!

I've just baked a batch of pretzels.

Cooking chaos
Unfortunately, Mia is better at burning cakes than baking them. Dog walking is definitely more her style!

Butterfly Beauty Shop

Whether the folks of Heartlake City need just a little beauty boost or a total style makeover, Sarah always has the answer at the Butterfly Beauty Shop. It's *the* place to go for head-to-toe pampering and grooming.

Wig shelf

This color will look perfect on you!

Sarah

Makeup palette

Style queue

Fashion-loving Emma
wouldn't trust anyone
but Sarah with her hair.
Sarah gets the style
right every time!

New look

The Butterfly Beauty
Shop also sells makeup.
When Emma wants a
new lip color, Sarah
knows exactly which
shade will suit her.

Water fountain

Advertisement

Finishing touches

Sarah thinks a look isn't
complete without an accessory.
She sells a range of bows, belts,
and purses to choose from.

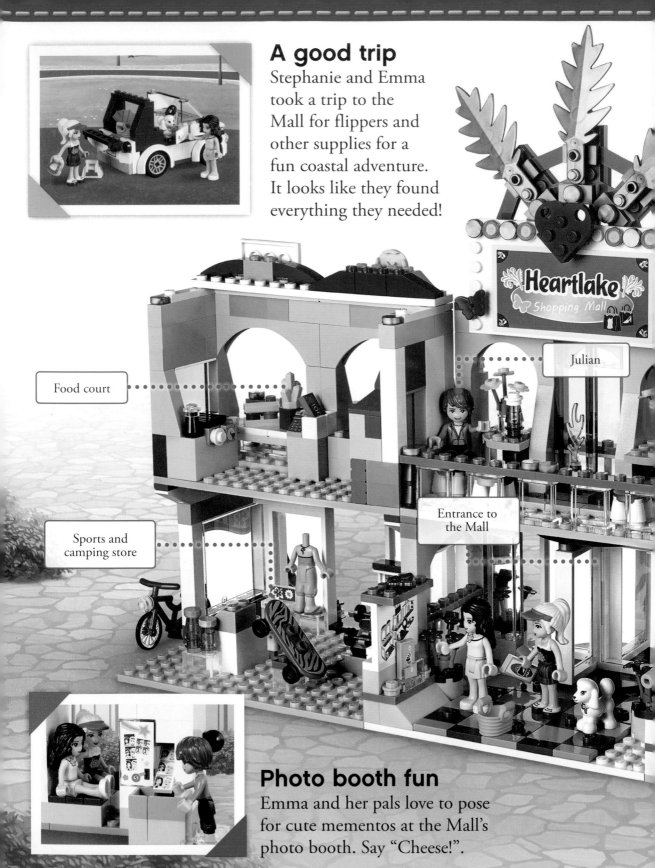

A good trip

Stephanie and Emma took a trip to the Mall for flippers and other supplies for a fun coastal adventure. It looks like they found everything they needed!

Heartlake
Shopping Mall

Food court

Julian

Sports and
camping store

Entrance to
the Mall

Photo booth fun

Emma and her pals love to pose for cute mementos at the Mall's photo booth. Say "Cheese!".

Heartlake Shopping Mall

Bridal boutique

Emma loves the Shopping Mall. She knows all the store owners, and visits every week to check out the new clothing styles. There are lots of wonderful shops to explore, a food court full of treats, a beauty spa for ultimate relaxation, and all kinds of fun events are held there, too.

Charity fashion show

The Mall recently hosted a charity show. Heartlake High students and their pets walked the runway. Emma swapped her camera for the DJ decks, while Julian took photos.

Beauty spa

119

Heartlake Vet

This friendly, modern surgery is where Heartlake City's sick and injured animals are taken to get well again. Animal-loving Mia volunteers here, helping Dr. Sophie, the veterinarian, in her spare time.

Weigh in
Sophie weighs all the animals regularly. They need to be fed a balanced diet to keep them fit, healthy, and happy.

Top secret!
Sophie, the vet, loves all animals, but her favorite animals are dogs.

New puppy patient coming in!

Rescue trolley

Mailbox

Busy surgery

When Sophie and Mia aren't treating animals, they book appointments and give advice over the phone.

Big and small

All kinds of animals are treated at the surgery. Large animals rest in a recovery stall, while smaller animals are looked after in the caged area next door.

Large animal stall

Medicine and medical equipment

Patient sign

Stethoscope

Cage for small animals

Heartlake Pet Salon

Now the pets of Heartlake City can get groomed and look gorgeous too. The Heartlake Pet Salon offers a range of special treatments, including shampoos, pedicures, and massages. Style-savvy Emma works there and her poodle, Lady, is her best customer!

Did you know?
Joanna and Emma both like art and design, so they love to experiment with new poodle fashions!

Pet food store

It's time for your makeover, Lady.

Emma chooses a purple bow from the accessories stand.

Water dish

Top team

Emma's friend, Joanna, works in the salon, too. First Emma washes Lady's coat, then Joanna blow-dries it.

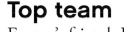
Blow-dry bar

Birdhouse

Doggy diva

Emma wants every pet to look and feel great: She trims, brushes, and styles Lady's coat. She's so pretty!

Good job!

Emma and Joanna enjoy everything about working at the Pet Salon. Well, apart from clipping dogs' toe nails!

Heartlake Stables

Mia visits her horse, Bella, every day at the Heartlake Stables. It's a busy place—horses need to be fed, groomed, watered, and exercised regularly. Katharina helps to train the horses, so she spends a lot of time here, too.

Grooming

Brushing Bella's coat keeps it clean and shiny. Mia also combs her mane and tail, and checks her hooves for stones.

Olivia's cat, Maxie, often hangs out here.

Pitchfork

Grooming equipment

Lunch time

Mia feeds Bella plenty of hay, and a carrot or two as a treat. She needs to be fit and strong for their next competition.

Chilling out

When the horses have been checked, Mia and Katharina relax in the hayloft by reading books about horses. They're both horse crazy!

Fresh water well

Top secret!

Mia thinks Katharina is the best rider she has ever seen. She hopes Katharina will give her riding tips one day.

Niki

Hay

Practice jumps

Heartlake Flying Club

Energetic Stephanie likes a challenge. She thought learning to fly would be exciting, so she joined the Heartlake Flying Club. Now she's earned her pilot's license, the sky's the limit for Stephanie!

Soaring high

Stephanie flies a seaplane, which can take off, land, and float on water.

Goldie watches the planes fly.

Club house

Club flag

Pier with mooring for planes

Planning a trip

Before Stephanie gets into her plane, she uses her map and telescope to plan her route carefully.

Flight details

Every pilot must record their flight details at the club house. Stephanie has done her flight plan and is good to go!

Propeller

Did you know?
Stephanie is the newest and the youngest member of the Heartlake Flying Club.

Cockpit

Float for takeoffs and landings on water

In training

Charlie has entered the agility competition. Mia is teaching him how to run over obstacles, such as the seesaw. He's so fast!

Looking good

Mia wants Charlie and Scarlett to look their best for the dog show. She gives Scarlett a bath to make sure her coat is super shiny.

Cupboard for grooming equipment

Good job, Scarlett.

Bone snacks

Heartlake Dog Show

The Heartlake Dog Show is the highlight of the canine calendar. It's a chance for Heartlake City's pooches to show off their talents. Mia has entered her puppy, Charlie, and Olivia's puppy, Scarlett, for the first time.

Winners' podium with prizes

Best in show

Clever Charlie and speedy Scarlett win first and second prize at the show. They both get purple ribbons, but Charlie also takes home a silver trophy.

Hurdle for dogs to jump over

Runway allows the judges to see the puppies in action

Fully equipped

The cozy Beach House has a kitchen for cooking up tasty treats, a power shower to wash off all the sand, and a terrace for soaking up the sun.

Home comforts

In fact, Stephanie's Beach House has everything she needs—there's even a TV and an MP3 player!

Outdoor steps to upper floor

Kate eating an ice cream

Beach House

During the summer, Stephanie loves to spend time at her family's Beach House, hanging out with her fun-loving friend Kate. Sometimes Stephanie stays there for days at a time, swimming, surfing, and snorkeling at the beach.

Palm tree.

Surf's up

This summer, Stephanie has been learning how to windsurf. Kate has given her some great beginners' tips.

Did you know?

Stephanie's friend, Kate, loves water sports. Her latest passion is diving.

MP3 player and speakers

Chilling out

Beach fans Stephanie and Kate agree on the best way to relax—with a yummy ice cream on the terrace.

131

Heartlake City Pool

Andrea loves to swim and play fun games at the Heartlake City Pool with her friend Isabella. This year Andrea also has a job: Selling ice cream at the pool's City Park Café refreshment stand.

City Park Café refreshment stand

Hot spot
The hot tub is Andrea and Isabella's favorite spot. The bubbles are so relaxing.

Shooting hoops
This summer Isabella and Andrea are learning how to play water basketball.

Picnic table

Diving board

Outdoor shower

The girls wash off all the sunscreen and chlorine from the pool before they head home.

Shower

Bathroom

The slide is so much fun!

Top secret!
Andrea dreams of putting on a poolside concert, but for now she just sings as she sells ice creams!

Sun lounger

Heartlake Horse Show

Stephanie and Robert work together to organize the annual Heartlake Horse Show. People come from all over the City to the fun event. This year, Stephanie has also entered a competition with Ruby, her favorite horse from the stables. Go Stephanie!

Competition time

Stephanie and Ruby have practiced the jumps many times, but doing it for real is much harder!

Did you know?
The Horse Show isn't just about competition. There are comedy skits and musical performances, too.

MAJOR   RUBY

Taking a break

Ruby has worked really hard. Stephanie makes sure she has plenty of water. She thinks Ruby deserves a tasty treat, too.

White horse logo

Winners' ribbons

I can't believe we won! Well done, Ruby!

Judging panel

Robert is judging one of the events. He's ready with his score, and thinks that Stephanie and Ruby have performed the best. They are the winners!

Heartlake City Horse Show trophy

Winners' podium

Heartlake Juice Bar

Heartlake City's healthiest new hangout is the Juice Bar. It's the place to go for a fresh juice or a vitamin-packed smoothie. Andrea is a regular customer—the healthy drinks help to keep her voice in top condition.

Creative Naya

Naya works at the Juice Bar. She wouldn't dare serve a drink that doesn't look beautiful—no matter how many people are waiting in line!

Decision time

Andrea's favorite juice is carrot and orange. It contains lots of vitamins A and C, which help keep away sore throats.

Drinks menu

Did you know?

As well as juices and smoothies, the Juice Bar serves sandwiches. Yum!

New friend

The Juice Bar is a great place to chat. Andrea has learned that Naya plays the saxophone. They're both music fans!

Smoothie maker

OPEN

Juicer

One strawberry smoothie coming up.

Fruit store

137

Sunshine Ranch

Summer is Mia's favorite season because she gets to spend time at her grandparents' farm, Sunshine Ranch. There are chickens to feed, vegetables to grow, and horses to groom and exercise. It's hard work, but Mia loves it all!

Journal hidden in secret loft space

En suite bathroom

Favorite cousin

Mia's cousin, Liza, often visits Sunshine Ranch. The two cousins have lots to catch up on. Liza loves to hear about Mia's adventures with Olivia, Andrea, Emma, and Stephanie.

Blaize and his newborn foal, Fame

Snack time

Mia and Liza help out with lots of jobs on the farm, but the busy girls always make sure they take regular snack breaks.

A basket of Liza's homegrown fruit and vegetables

Happy horses

Mia spends as much time as she can with the horses. While she grooms Mocca, Liza plans what to write in her journal.

Mocca waiting to be groomed

Did you know?
Mia first learned to ride horses on Blaize at Sunshine Ranch.

Jungle Rescue Base

Top secret!

Olivia is not just learning about animals at the Rescue Base, it has also given her some cool ideas for her tree house back home.

Radio antenna

Deep in the heart of the jungle, Andrea, Stephanie, Mia, Olivia, and Emma are on a mission—to help Dr. Sophie rescue endangered animals. The girls are staying at a fantastic base, built amongst the trees. It has a watchtower for looking out for animals in danger and a medical center, too.

Winch and rope

Java at the lookout post

Zip wire

Jungle vines

Freshwater inlet

Slide

Poor panda

Bamboo has been scratched by a nasty animal. Stephanie and Andrea use the Rescue Base medical equipment to clean him up and check his injuries.

River emergency!

Stephanie has had a radio call from Mia in the helicopter. There's a tiger in trouble! Stephanie goes down the slide to the rescue boat. Tony the chameleon is coming, too.

Skylight

Living quarters and medical center

Living quarters

Being in charge of the Rescue Base is hard work. The girls cook and eat dinner with the animals, before finally heading to bed.

Vehicles

Whether it's by land, sea, or air, Olivia, Stephanie, Andrea, Mia, and Emma always travel in style. They love being able to go where they want, when they want, especially if it turns into a fun girls' road trip!

Hop in! Where shall we go today?

Stephanie's Convertible

Stephanie is always planning parties, sleepovers, and adventures, so she often needs to get somewhere in a hurry. That's when she jumps into her cool convertible. It's a fast car, but don't worry—Stephanie's a very safe driver!

Taking pride
She's a busy girl, but Stephanie always makes time to clean her car. Her neighbor's dog, Coco, helps out, too.

Coco's grooming kit

Cool starburst design on the hood

Top secret!
Stephanie delivers cupcakes in her car. She watches cake decorating videos on repeat to learn new techniques.

Driving mirror

Headlights

144

Olivia's Speedboat

While Stephanie zooms around the streets of Heartlake City, Olivia prefers to make waves on the deep blue ocean. This speedboat belongs to her parents, but Olivia has their permission to take it out whenever she likes.

Summer fun

After a cruise around the bay in the speedboat, Olivia likes to relax on the beach. What a perfect summer's day!

Did you know?
Andrea also prefers boats to cars. She heads out on the ocean in her very own boat.

I hope I spot some turtles!

Life buoy

Driver's seat

Windshield

Adventure Camper

Life in Heartlake City is fabulous, but Olivia also likes to explore the countryside as often as she can. When nature calls, Olivia heads out on the open road for an adventure in her friend Nicole's camper van.

Camp cook out

Outdoor adventures are hungry work, so Olivia and Nicole cook up a feast on the outdoor grill. Watch out for bears!

Unique heart and flower logo

What's over the next mountain?

Super-charged headlights

Day trip

Olivia's favorite way of exploring the countryside is by bike. The girls can cycle for miles, so Olivia always packs a picnic to share.

Chilling out

The camper van has plenty of home comforts, including a TV. Well, Nicole and Olivia need to relax after a full day of adventuring!

TV aerial

Bike and surfboard in trailer

The side opens to keep the girls cool when they hang out in the van.

Top secret!

Once, Olivia completely forgot to attach the trailer. She had to drive back to fetch it. Oops!

Pet Patrol

Stephanie loves riding her ATV (all-terrain vehicle), but it isn't just for fun. She often patrols Heartlake City on it, looking for lost or injured animals to help. The vehicle has sturdy wheels for off-road riding and a trailer for carrying rescued animals and food.

Rabbit rescue

Stephanie returns lost pets to their homes and takes sick or wounded animals to Sophie, the vet. This rabbit had no owner, so Stephanie took her home to look after her. She named her Daisy.

Did you know?
Energetic Stephanie is learning to be calmer and quieter as she sometimes frightens the animals!

Big tires for bumpy terrain

Rabbit food—hay and carrots

Olivia's Ice-Cream Bike

When Olivia found a rusty old bike, it gave her a fantastic idea for a summer business—a mobile ice-cream stall. So, practical Olivia fixed up the bike, then added a cooler, a stand, and an umbrella. This might be Olivia's coolest invention yet!

First customer

Olivia tests her new ice-cream flavors on her friends. They think they're delicious. Andrea's favorite is Berry Surprise.

Hand painted sign

Olivia's shiny red bike

Top secret!
Olivia has invented her own unique ice-cream flavors, including Lemon Swirl, Chocolate Explosion, and Berry Surprise.

Cooler

149

Emma's Horse Trailer

Although Emma's passion is for design, she thinks horses are thrilling too. She travels to show jumping competitions with her horse, Robin, and, of course, they always go in style. Their truck and trailer are the prettiest on the road!

Horse treats
Emma always keeps a fresh supply of snacks for Robin, but Robin prefers to eat the flowers!

Open-top truck

Best friends
Emma loves riding Robin, but she also likes braiding his hair in cool ways to create new styles.

Personalized license plate

Show time!

Robin likes being led into his luxurious trailer after shows. It's so comfortable, and he loves to feel the wind through the open window.

Did you know?
Emma painted the horse and butterfly design on the side of the trailer.

Rear light

Window

Sturdy wheels

Ramp can be lowered to let Robin in and out

151

Summer Caravan

Olivia adores camping and this summer she is doing it in style. Her new caravan is like a beautiful little house on wheels! She can hitch it to her new, color-coordinated convertible and head out anywhere. Her friend Joanna is joining her for an amazing adventure.

Home comforts
Olivia's caravan has a tiny kitchen and a cozy bed. It's so cozy that cheeky Oscar, the hedgehog, has snuck inside for a nap!

Matching convertible

Outside lamp

Seeing stars

On warm nights, Olivia loves to open up the roof and gaze at the stars. She shows Joanna her favorite constellation—Ursa Major, or the Great Bear. Awesome!

Day trip

A great thing about the caravan is that Olivia can park it safely in a field and then head out in her convertible. Joanna wants to take a trip to go hiking.

Removable roof

Striped awning

Dolphin Cruiser

Mia is passionate about helping animals, so she can't wait to climb aboard the *Dolphin Cruiser*. Mia, Maya, and Andrew are on a mission to study the dolphins in the ocean. They plan to have some fun, too!

Searching the ocean

The *Dolphin Cruiser* has special sonar equipment to locate dolphins underwater. Maya and Andrew like to have a drink at the snack bar and listen for any dolphins.

Letting go

After a busy day studying marine life, Mia and Maya have found the perfect way to relax—a thrilling water slide. It goes straight into the ocean!

Picnic area

I think I see dolphins, guys!

Sun lounger

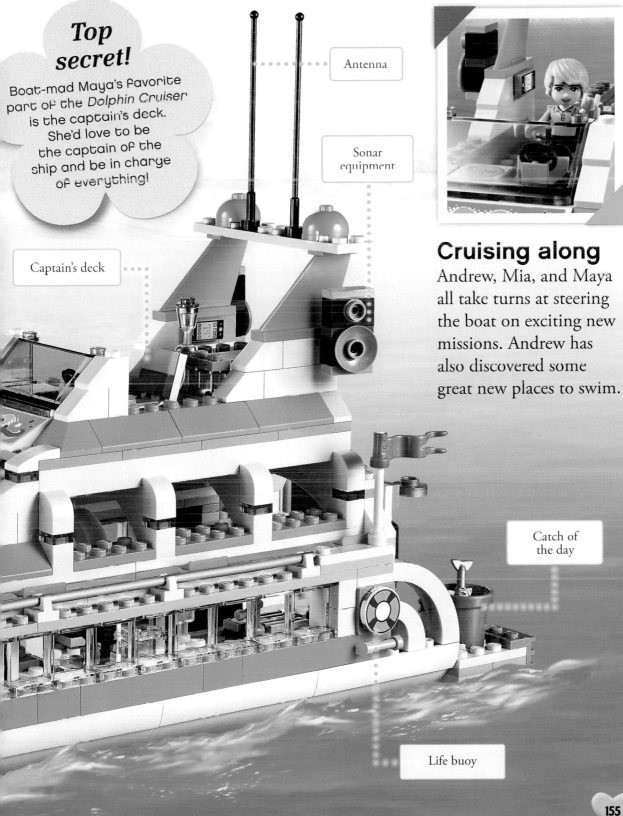

Antenna

Sonar equipment

Captain's deck

Cruising along

Andrew, Mia, and Maya all take turns at steering the boat on exciting new missions. Andrew has also discovered some great new places to swim.

Catch of the day

Life buoy

Olivia's Beach Buggy

When she's not busy inventing things in her workshop, Olivia enjoys zooming up and down the sand dunes of Ambersands Beach in her customized beach buggy. She likes to practice her surfing, so she takes her board on the ride, too.

Surf's up!

Olivia's grandmother gave her a surfboard and surf lessons for her birthday. Olivia was unsure at first, but soon became hooked!

Olivia modified the buggy so it could hold a surfboard.

Did you know?
Olivia bought a beat-up beach buggy and then rebuilt it herself. She added a few new features, too.

Off-road tires

Olivia painted the buggy purple.

156

Sports Car

Stephanie told Emma driving was fun, and she was right! Emma loves loading her cat, Jewel, into her new sports car and heading off for an adventure. She always takes her camera, in case she finds design inspiration, and a map, in case she gets lost.

Scenic spot

Emma often drives to the Clearspring Mountains. She and Jewel stop for a picnic and enjoy amazing views of the bay.

Let's go on a fabulous adventure!

Top secret!
It took Emma three attempts to pass her driving test. But she is an excellent driver now!

Spacious trunk

Star decoration

Jewel

Wing mirror

157

News Van

Emma is always finding ways to use her creative talents. From fashion to design, all her projects are aimed at making Heartlake City even more fabulous. Emma's latest project is the Heartlake High TV station, bringing students news stories from a mobile TV studio in the hi-tech news van.

Behind the news

Andrew helps Emma to drive the van around Heartlake City and put together all the breaking news stories.

Weather report

Emma enjoys reading the weather. It's often sunny in Heartlake City, but it can be a bit breezy down on the seafront. Hold on to your hats!

Cooking up a story

Today's big scoop is about the world's prettiest cake, which has been baked in Heartlake City. It has all the ingredients for a great news story!

Satellite dish ......

Desk holds special makeup to wear on TV. .....

TV monitors

Top secret!
Sometimes Andrew thinks he would prefer to be in front of the camera. He is secretly a bit jealous of Emma!

Computer

The side of the van opens to reveal the TV studio.

Revolving chair

Sunshine Harvest Tractor

Roll up, roll up!

Olivia sells the Ranch's fresh fruit and vegetables, plus jars of Mia's grandmother's homemade jellies and pickles on a stall at the market. It's very popular with the regulars.

Olivia loves to help out at Sunshine Ranch, but it's hard work. First she has to pick the apples and strawberries, and then she must take them to market. Driving the tractor is a lot of fun, though!

Charlie in the trailer

Exhaust pipe

Sturdy wheels for off-road driving

Did you know?
Olivia is allowed to keep 10% of all the profits from the stall. She's saving up to buy new parts for Zobo, her robot.

Jungle Bridge Rescue Helicopter

In the jungle, Mia and her friends have to figure out everything—including who will pilot the awesome rescue helicopter! A poor bear needs rescuing from a rickety rope bridge. What a test of skill! Can Mia do it?

Headphones

Winch

Top secret!
Stephanie, Mia, and Robert argue over who gets to fly the rescue helicopter.

Protective basket for Blu the bear

Up in the air

Brave Mia would do anything to help an animal. She packs her walkie-talkie and heads for the cockpit. It's time to fly.

Jungle Bridge Rescue Truck

Traveling through the dense jungle is not always easy because there aren't many roads. Matthew has found the perfect transport solution—this heavy-duty, off-road vehicle. Its sturdy tires can cope with any terrain!

Teamwork

While Matthew looks for injured animals on the ground, Mia searches from the sky. The intrepid rescuers keep in contact via walkie-talkies.

Did you know?
The rescue truck can even drive through shallow water. Matthew loves making a big splash!

Medical logo

Medical supplies

Windshield protects against branches and bugs

All-terrain tires

RS 036

First Aid Jungle Bike

When an animal is in distress, the gang might not have much time to save them. Fortunately, Emma has a speedy and reliable mode of transportation—a motorcycle. Don't worry Juliet, Emma is coming to rescue you!

Mobile medication

Emma's motorcycle carries injured animals, such as Juliet the orangutan, in the sidecar. She also has a medical kit so she can give first aid on the spot.

Walkie-talkie

Mobile medical kit

Top secret!

At first, Emma was scared of patroling the jungle by herself, but she overcame her fears when she saw how much the animals needed her.

Off-road tire

Detachable sidecar

Mini-doll Gallery

The LEGO® Friends mini-dolls have many different stylish outfits. There have been more than 80 mini-dolls so far, with more than 50 fabulous versions of Mia, Olivia, Emma, Andrea, and Stephanie, and more than 30 mini-dolls of their family and friends.

Olivia
(Olivia's Tree House)

Olivia p6
(Adventure Camper, Olivia's House, Desk)

Olivia
(2012 Advent Calendar)

Olivia
(Olivia's Inventor Workshop)

Mia
(Heartlake Dog Show)

Mia
(Mia's Magic Tricks)

Mia
(Downtown Bakery)

Mia
(Dolphin Cruiser)

Emma
(Heartlake Pet Salon)

Emma
(Emma's Sports Car)

Emma
(Emma's Lifeguard Post)

Emma
(Heartlake News Van)

Emma
(Heartlake Shopping Mall)

Emma
(First Aid Jungle Bike)

Stephanie p9
(Heartlake Flying Club, Mailbox, Stephanie's Cool Convertible)

Stephanie
(Summer Riding Camp)

Stephanie
(Stephanie's Outdoor Bakery)

Stephanie
(Stephanie's Pet Patrol)

Andrea
(Andrea's Stage)

Andrea
(Andrea's Bunny House)

Andrea
(Heartlake City Pool)

Andrea
(Andrea's Bedroom)

Andrea
(Heartlake Juice Bar)

Andrea
(Andrea's Mountain Hut)

Andrea
(Jungle Rescue Base)

Kate p11
(Water Scooter Fun)

Kate
(Stephanie's Beach House)

Andrew p
(Dolphin Cruiser)

Katharina p21
(Heartlake Stables)

Lily p22
(2013 Advent Calendar)

Isabella p23
(Heartlake City Pool)

Julian p24
(Heartlake Shopping Mall)

Ewa p25
(2014 Advent Calendar)

Naya p26
(Heartlake Juice Bar)

Naya
(comes with the trade edition of this book)

Robert p27
(Heartlake Horse Show)

Joanna p28
(Heartlake Pet Salon)

Joanna
(Summer Caravan)

Olivia
(Olivia's Speedboat)

Olivia
(Olivia's Newborn Foal)

Olivia
(Olivia's Beach Buggy, Jungle Boat)

Olivia
(Sunshine Harvest)

Olivia
(Olivia's Ice-Cream Bike)

Olivia
(Jungle Falls Rescue)

Olivia
(Summer Caravan)

Mia p7
(Heartlake Vet, Heartlake Stables, Mia's Skateboard, Summer Picnic, DK LEGO Friends Brickmaster)

Mia
(Mia's Puppy House)

Mia
(Mia's Bedroom)

Mia
(Mia's Lemonade Stand)

Mia
(Sunshine Ranch)

Mia
(2014 Advent Calendar)

Mia
(Jungle Bridge Rescue)

Mia
(Jungle Tree Sanctuary)

Emma
(Emma's Design Studio)

Emma p8
(Butterfly Beauty Shop, Car, Ice Cream Stand, Summer Riding Camp)

Emma
(Emma's Horse Trailer)

Emma
(Emma's Splash Pool)

Emma
(Emma's Karate Class)

Stephanie
(Rehearsal Stage)

Stephanie
(Heartlake High)

Stephanie
(Stephanie's Soccer Practice)

Stephanie
(2013 Advent Calendar)

Stephanie
(Stephanie's Newborn Lamb)

Stephanie
(Stephanie's Beach House)

Stephanie
(Heartlake Horse Show)

Stephanie
(Heartlake Shopping Mall)

Stephanie
(Jungle Rescue Base)

Andrea p10
(City Park Café, Beach, Birthday Party)

Andrew
(Heartlake City News Van)

Ella p13
(Summer Riding Camp)

Liza p14
(Sunshine Ranch)

Maya p15
(Dolphin Cruiser)

Christina p16
(2012 Advent Calendar)

Chloe p17
(DK LEGO Friends Brickmaster)

Nicole p18
(Adventure Camper)

Matthew p19
(Heartlake High)

Matthew
(Jungle Bridge Rescue)

Danielle p20
(Downtown Bakery)

Sarah p29
(Butterfly Beauty Shop)

Anna p30
(Olivia's House)

Peter p31
(Olivia's House)

Dr. Sophie p32
(Heartlake Vet)

Dr. Sophie
(Heartlake Shopping Mall)

Ms. Stevens p33
(Heartlake High)

Theresa p34
(Summer Riding Camp)

Marie p35
(City Park Café)

Animal Gallery

The LEGO® Friends all love animals and many sets wouldn't be complete without a cute pet or exotic creature. So far, there are more horses than any other animal. The range of cute jungle dwellers varies from an orangutan to a chameleon!

Scarlett p43
(Heartlake Vet,
Heartlake Dog Show,
Stephanie's Soccer
Practice)

Charlie p46
(Mia's Puppy House,
Heartlake Dog Show,
Sunshine Harvest)

Celie p59
(Poodle's Litt
Palace)

Daisy p41
(Stephanie's Pet Patrol,
Mia's Magic Tricks,
Sunshine Ranch)

Lucky p77
(Bunny's Hutch)

Jazz p48
(Andrea's Bunn
House)

Champion p62
(Summer Riding Camp)

Foxie p62
(Summer Riding Camp)

Sunshine p65
(Summer Riding Camp)

Snow p65
(Olivia's Newborn Foa

Cotton p80
(Stephanie's
Newborn Lamb)

Clara p55
(Sunshine Ranch)

Cream p64
(Sunshine Ranch)

Jojo p40
(Hedgehog's
Hideaway)

Oscar p40
(Summer Riding Camp,
Heartlake Vet, Summer
Caravan)

Goldie p42
(Heartlake Flying Club,
Olivia's Tree House,
Jungle Tree Sanctuary)

Hoo p67
(Heartlake Hig

Satin p71
(Seal's Little Rock)

Casper p69
(Penguin's
Playground)

Java p53
(Macaw's Fountain,
Jungle Rescue Base)

Plum p68
(Turtle's Little
Paradise)

Bubbles p45
(Turtle's Little Oasis,
Jungle Tree Sanctuary)

Tony p63
(Jungle Falls Rescue,
Jungle Rescue Base)

Zip p81
(Jungle Boat, Jung
Bridge Rescue, Jung
Rescue Base)

Coco p54
(Stephanie's Cool Convertible, 2012 Advent Calendar)

Max p78
(Puppy's Playhouse)

Lady p72
(Heartlake Pet Salon, Heartlake Shopping Mall)

Maxie p39
(Olivia's Tree House, Heartlake Stables, Sunshine Ranch)

Jewel p57
(Emma's Sports Car, 2014 Advent Calendar)

Kitty p60
(Olivia's House)

Felix p74
(Cat's Playground)

Robin p44
(Emma's Horse Trailer)

Bella p38
(Heartlake Vet, Heartlake Stables)

Major p56
(Heartlake Horse Show)

Ruby p56
(Heartlake Horse Show)

Niki p75
(Heartlake Stables)

Blaize p79
(Sunshine Ranch)

Mocca p79
(Sunshine Ranch)

Fame p79
(Sunshine Ranch)

Kiki p58
(Parrot's Perch)

Hazel p52
(2013 Advent Calendar, Squirrel's Tree House, Andrea's Mountain Hut)

Misty p49
(Fawn's Forest, 2014 Advent Calendar)

Sheen p51
(Dolphin Cruiser)

Milo p51
(Dolphin Cruiser, Emma's Lifeguard Post)

Juliet p47
(Orangutan's Banana Tree, First Aid Jungle Bike, Jungle Tree Sanctuary)

Romeo p76
(Jungle Rescue Base)

Bobbi p61
(Lion Cub's Savanna, Jungle Tree Sanctuary)

Flame p73
(Tiger's Beautiful Temple, Jungle Falls Rescue)

Bamboo p66
(Jungle Rescue Base, Panda's Bamboo)

Blu p50
(Jungle Bridge Rescue)

Biscuit p70
(Brown Bear's River)

Accessories

The LEGO® Friends need a variety of tools and equipment for their part-time jobs, hobbies, and their animals. Of course, they have lots of fabulous fashion accessories, too.

Brushes

Fish

Milk bottle

Scissors

Bowl

Water spray bottle

Sports and hobbies

Riding hat

Flippers

Basketball

Magician's wand

Magician's cards

Oilcan

Soccer ball

Skis

Karate helmet

Telescope

Science beaker

Map

Trophies

Technology

Microphone

Camera

Cell phone

Laptop